Sri M said,
the 'parikrama' was not complete
with the end of the Yatra;
it should be continued in our
everyday life with the same fervor
and equanimity as one adopted
during the 'parikrama' to Kailash.
The Yatra had indeed introduced
a novel dimension to our
perceptions of life.
We looked forward to the dawn of a newer
insight into life
and the way we lived it.

Kailash-Manasarovar Yatra

A Journey with Sri M

Dr. Nayana Kashyap

Magenta Press

First Published: 2014
Second Reprint: 2022

ISBN: 978-93-82585-11-4

Book design: J. Menon. www.grantha.com

Published by:
Magenta Press and Publication Pvt Ltd.,
No.9,1st Floor, Websters Road, Cox Town
Bengaluru – 560005,Karnataka, India
Tel: +91 9343071537 / 6363083590
info@magentapress.in / www.magentapress.in

A sapphire expanse of serene water girdled by a string of mountains revealed itself to us at the end of an arduous journey for thousands of kilometers away from home. The placid waves of the mythical Manasarovar lapped on its banks complementing the wonder in our hearts that we were by its side at last! To its right, stood the magnificent Mt. Kailash, occasionally obscured by the floating fog. An air of dreaminess enveloped us; we were in this world and yet far away from it. In the lap of pristine, pure nature our spirits felt exalted. The confluence with nature was so complete that tears rolled down many a cheek, unawares. There stood Mahadeva, a witness to all. Beside us stood Sri M, witnessing the witness with his moist eyes, and then prostrating himself before Him in all humility.

As Sri M narrated in one of the Satsangs during the yatra, he had to wait for forty long years to visit the place after his first attempt was thwarted by ill health when he was just about twenty. It was perhaps his master Babaji's prophecy that he would one day reach the place with a large group of people, which stalled him from embarking on the journey alone.

Sri M's benevolence in preparing us all for the yatra had begun to flow right from 2006 when he expressed his wish to make a trip to Kailash-Manasarovar. No one gave it a serious thought at the time; although many of us resolved to join him in the journey whenever it would be. For all of us going on a pilgrimage to Mt. Kailash with Sri M was of primary concern rather than the pilgrimage itself.

For three years there was no mention of the yatra in any of Sri M's satsangs or retreats. Then suddenly in December 2008 at a retreat in Sadum, Sri M nonchalantly announced that it will be flagged off in July 2009! The plan was now truly in motion.

Preparations for the much awaited yatra with Sri M to Mt. Kailash virtually began when an email address was created to co-ordinate potential participants. The organizers anticipated a wide and varied pool of enthusiasts from around the world. The formal enrolment began. In less than a month, the list carried a whopping fifty names with some more of them still pouring in! Finally the confirmed entries closed at fifty seven. Sri M decided that the yatra should commence on July 2nd and the itinerary was planned accordingly.

The months from January to June flew by meeting the requirements for the yatra like paying up the advance, the airfare, payment of the final amount, buying necessary clothes and climbing accessories, informing family, friends and colleagues about our future absence for a whole 17 days. By the third week of June an anxious countdown began and so did the packing. Our requirements for the trip were packed in red, numbered cargo bags provided by the tour agency. As a result, all through the yatra except during the Kailash parikrama, we were accompanied by a large mass of bright red bags!

DAY 1:

The yatra began on 2nd July at 4.30 a.m. The yatris from in and around Bangalore left for the airport all together in a bus arranged by the travel agent. As the day quietly broke, the disposition of the yatris was ambivalent with excitement, angst, and anticipation about the days to come. At 6.45 a.m. the Bangalore group boarded the Delhi bound flight. Although Sri M was to travel with us there was no sign of him until we occupied our seats. He then made a silent, smiling entry into the aircraft! A smile shone on the countenance of every yatri on seeing him. The aircraft took off into the lofty plane of creamy clouds and soon after the seatbelt sign was turned off, Sri M walked up to every yatri to exchange cheer and a few words.

At Delhi's Indira Gandhi International Airport, yatris from Chennai and Delhi joined us and at 12 pm we boarded the flight to Katmandu. We experienced the delight of catching the first glimpse of the snow-capped peaks of the Himalayan range in just an hour after the aircraft took off. As we flew closer to Katmandu, a verdant green world patterned with fields and brick houses spread out below us. A panoramic view of the enchanting beauty of the hills and forests of Nepal encouraged us to expect more of nature's bounty in the ensuing days.

At 2 in the afternoon, a modest brick structure bearing the name 'Tribhuvan International Airport' welcomed us to the Hindu-Buddhist country of Nepal. At the passport checking counter, we had to specify that we were heading to Kailash-

Manasarovar without conveying which our passports wouldn't be stamped!

From the airport, we were driven in two buses to Park village Resort and Spa. It was already nearing three o'clock and all of us were famished. When finally we reached the sprawling resort, we proceeded straight to the dining hall! A few members of our group, who had already reached Katmandu on their own, were awaiting the group there. Only after lunch we checked into our rooms which were spread out across the resort and bore names of flowers and trees. Sri M stayed at the Maple House. The day had begun early and hence everyone needed a good nap.

At 5pm we emerged from our cozy rooms, had tea, and took a walk up to the temple of Buddha Neelkanth, which was about a kilometer and a half from the hotel. The ancient idol in supine, cross-legged position in the centre of the temple pond is atypical by its concept of Vishnu (resting on Seshnag), Krishna (a peacock feather in the crown), Shiva (a snake on the arm), and Buddha (long ears) – all integrated into one! The atmosphere was filled with the sound of bhajans, visitors, beggars, and sadhus – and was for us a new and fresh ambiance.

After this brief taste of Katmandu we returned to our resort for a preparatory address by Sri M. He suggested some useful, practical tips to be adopted during the yatra, especially during the three day parikrama. The tour operator too added some helpful information about what can be and cannot be expected during the yatra. The rest of the day was meant for relaxation.

DAY 2:

Several early birds, including Sri M of course, went for a morning walk, some in small groups; some on their own. Then, after a refreshing shower and a satisfying breakfast, we headed out into Katmandu for sightseeing in three mini buses. Some way into the tour, we alighted from the buses and entered a '*mahadwar*'. We were fascinated by two large, benign eyes painted slightly stretched wide in a stylized manner, at the top of the mammoth Baudhanath Stupa. Walking around the circumference of the dome-shaped stupa, rotating the prayer wheels set around it, we came across the Baudhanath Temple situated directly in front of the over-watching wide eyes in which a large idol of Buddha resided. The air was abuzz with the Pali chants of Buddhist monks, the sounds of trade and amusement, of faith and oddity!

Our next destination was the famed Pashupatinath Temple before visiting which we were asked to visit the smaller temples on the premises, of Vasuki Nagraj, of reclining Narayana, of a maze of innumerable *lingas*, of Sri Yantra on the banks of the river Bagmati, and of Kal Bhairav. The day of our visit was the special day of '*bada ekadashi*' and the place was teeming with Nepalese all dressed in varied shades of red, a mark of festivity and custom in Nepal.

In the afternoon, the group had another briefing by some more tour co-ordinators (chaotic at first but became purposeful after Sri M's intervention). The co-ordinators sold us Chinese Yuan for Indian rupees to be used in China after crossing the Nepal border. We were also advised to hire a down-jacket each since our warm clothes would not be adequate as the temperatures became extreme.

The evening was free for shopping and packing our backpack with only the most essential things. We retired early, as the next day's journey to Nyalam via Kodari, would begin at 6 am and was anticipated to be a long and tiring one.

DAY 3:

It was a momentous day; we were crossing over from Nepal into China Occupied Tibet via the Friendship Bridge at Kodari, about 200 kilometers from Katmandu. The uniqueness of the place made the drive exceptionally pleasant. All along the snaky roads, River Kosi flowed with us. Wayside motels, industrious women we met on the way, heaped pebbles, corn drying on strings hanging from the roofs of houses, resorts with signboards reading 'Food, Drink, Sound' – everything reflected the pluralism and multiplicity in the lifestyle of Nepalese masses. Nature and the ways and variety of human life unfurling before our eyes kept us all quiet and contemplative.

With the passage of Khadichaur, a hamlet, we were getting closer to Tibet and China and witnessed the bizarre co-existence of Buddhists and Maoists. A fleet of trucks parked in a yard off the road apparently belonged to the Maoist insurgents as one of the trucks had the face of the Chilean communist-activist Che Guevara painted on it!

Along the way, in some spots our buses had to slow down to wade through the huge boulders that had rolled down in heavy landslides. The route from Katmandu to Kodari was punctuated by such landslides, green mountains and plunging waterfalls. Before reaching the Friendship Bridge we crossed many smaller ones like Chaku Bridge and Phulping Bridge and arrived in Pattopani village where we stopped for lunch in a hotel. This was followed by a post-lunch, up-hill walk for about 1.5 kms to reach the Friendship Bridge at 1.30 pm Indian time (4 pm China time).

The process of passport and baggage checking of the entire group at the Chinese Immigration Bureau took more than an hour. Each of us had to pass through an infrared machine that detected increased body temperature, a sign of H1N1 virus, so as to avert its potential infiltration into China. Some members of our group who had the U.S. passport were put through a brief medical examination. Some others were also examined as their temperatures had risen after the up hill walk to the Bridge. Noticing that the rest of the group was anxious about the results of the test, for a couple of yatris were actually running fever, Sri M smilingly said that they would all come out clear. And so they did!

At 5.30 pm (China time), we got into the Toyota Land-Cruisers that were waiting for us outside the Immigration Bureau. Throughout the yatra, up to Yamadwar and from Manasarovar on the way back, until we returned to this place, we had to use the same vehicle which we boarded here. We were not allowed to switch between them for whatever reason as the drivers, knowing no other language than Tibetan, could identify their passengers only by face. Each vehicle carried four of us and the driver. The vehicles looked rickety and unmaintained from the outside, but were fairly tidy and comfortable inside and had exceptional pick-up.

The drive to Nyalam, the first Tibetan-Chinese town we were going to stay at, seemed infinite due to recurrent stops for reasons we were initially unable to ascertain. Later, of course, we came to know that the Chinese Military Police, who oversaw the road work that was undergoing, permitted vehicles to pass only in batches. Hence our convoy too was stopped every half an hour. Our initial annoyance, once we got used to these stops, disappeared and we began to even enjoy them! We made the most of them by hopping out of the vehicle, clicking photographs of the scenic beauty and people around, joking, laughing; and hopping in again once the vehicles were given the green signal.

After the first quarter of the stretch to Nyalam the roads were implausibly neat and wide enough for two vehicles to pass effortlessly. The exquisite drive into the clouds and sometimes beneath waterfalls was fantastic. It was like a drive into the Heavens with the sky-scraping, misty mountains receiving us into their fold. To add to this harmony and other-worldliness, our driver Patto played some gentle Tibetan music at just the apt volume that blended flawlessly well with the serenity around. Sri M's vehicle was speeding up in front of ours and in the twilight we could see his silhouetted form at every turn of the road. As we drove higher and higher into the mountains, the temperature began to plummet. One by one our warm clothes were pulled out of our backpack until we were completely enveloped.

We reached Nyalam situated at a height of 12,200 ft; at 9.30 pm. Darkness had only just begun to fall as the sun begins to set only after 9 pm in China! Our journey that day had commenced at 6 am (Nepal time) and ended at 9.30 pm (China time)! Indeed, a long day it was, but an impressive one! It was a flight from civilization and population to pristine nature with few inhabitants.

We alighted from our vehicles adapting our eyes to the murky darkness and dim lights of Nyalam Recreation Resort. We occupied the cots in the allotted mud houses whose interior was stunning with distinctive Tibetan drawings and wood work in vibrant colors. After our stay in the resort at Katmandu, this was a pleasant and unexpected change. But an awful fact was lurking in the dark! We soon discovered that the toilets were but open pits without an enclosure!! We were horrified; but Sri M found it only too funny to be troubled! Later, we chanced upon a comparatively cleaner 'toilet' which was a great collective relief.

The Sherpas functioning as cooks and transporters for the group had got into our buses at different points in Katmandu and had traveled with us through the day. Yet, in barely an hour after we reached, they came all set to serve us freshly prepared '*poha*' for dinner, inside the mud houses. However, Sri M chose to not wait for dinner that night and had gone to sleep without it. All of us were served poha and then Diamox, a pill that helped us breathe with less effort, as dessert! Thereafter, every morning and night after food, one of the Sherpa-cooks would dole out to us a half or one full pill of

Diamox, according to our need. This continued till our return to Nyalam, after the yatra to Kailash. The pill is consumed at high altitude where the atmosphere contains less oxygen, to dilate the blood vessel that supplies oxygen to the brain and assist a free flow of it.

We retired for the day huddled up in thick blankets inside the snug row of mud houses nestled amidst towering mountains in an alien land; far away from our homes, physically and mentally.

What divine sleep we enjoyed that night!

DAY 4:

We continued to stay in Nyalam even on the following day, for acclimatization. The Sherpas gave a wake up knock on our doors when they came to serve tea at 6 am. Sipping hot tea, we admired the gradual breaking of dawn, with the tender rays of the sun designing a light and shadow play on the lofty mountains right outside our mud houses.

Breakfast was served at 8.30. There was no question of having a bath. There was neither water nor bathrooms although it was called a resort! However, most of us were disinclined to take a bath since it was very cold. We felt we were pretty fresh!

Around 9.30 we started on a trial trek that was designed to gauge our abilities to walk and ascend at such high altitude. Though a few of our friends lagged behind, eventually everyone could make it to the near-top spot where we stopped. Here we relaxed on the rocks and engaged in some photography.

We made our way down watchfully. While some people went straight back to the resort, others stopped at a small hotel and ordered tea and *momos*, a local delicacy. The tea arrived promptly but the momos seemed to take endless time to get ready. A couple of youth in our group entered into the kitchen to help the lone lady cook who was striving to make momos for so many of us. But this didn't seem to help as the momos, we were informed, were still in the oven. It was already 12.45 pm. Sri M suggested that while the rest of us carried on, one could stay back to collect the packed momos that can be had with lunch. At 1 pm hot lunch comprising *dal* and potato along with rice, *roti*, and pickle arrived outside the mud house complex. During the lunch, finally the momos appeared only to disappear in a jiffy!

An evening *satsang* was suggested which Sri M consented to. It was to be held at 5.30. Till then we were free to explore the little town of Nyalam. The market sold some interesting stuff like mountaineering-accessories, some unusual warm clothes, china, and differently wrought thermos and so on. However, to purchase anything we had to bargain heavily. It was an extraordinary bargain as we did it through calculator due to the language barrier. If the shopkeeper entered her/his price, we typed ours. If it was objectionable the response would be a furious shake of the head; if it was reasonable, you got a quick nod from the shopkeeper. The deal was made!

The walk downtown was, in fact, excruciating due to innumerable pot holes, open man holes, and filth and slush all over. One had to literally wrap the face to be protected from dust and stench. Amidst this, a few tender hands would come stretching to you asking for '*churi*' and '*bindi*'. The poor young girls in Nyalam begged you for nothing but these two things! After a nippy walk in the town we returned to our dorms. We found that a member of our group, out on a similar walk had had a terrible fall. She suffered some cuts in the upper lip and bruises on the face. The doctor couple in the group diligently attended to her and saw to her swift recovery.

The satsang was to be held in the ladies dormitory. We happily tidied up the place in an instant. Everyone gathered there after tea. The tour coordinators too eagerly joined the group. The satsang at Nyalam, in fact, oriented our minds to understand the implications of the pilgrimage we had embarked on. Sri M drew our attention to the sanctity of the pilgrimage undertaken by thousands of people from centuries. Such a pilgrimage must be accomplished with a spirit of humility, he said.

He narrated how at the age of twenty he had attempted a trip to Mount Kailash. The attempt was interrupted by sickness and fever. Concerned about his health, Babaji had tied him to a yak and returned him to the safety of the lowlands. On recovery, when Sri M expressed his wish to resume the yatra, Babaji had advised him to visit the holy place after some years. Those were the times when Sri M was a wandering 'sadhak'. Both food and shelter were luxuries seldom available. He had to make do with what he could find. Sri M told us this to make us aware of the comforts we enjoyed now even in that hilly territory; to remind that we were far from being wandering 'sadhaks' since all our needs were easily met.

Sri M suggested that we try to spend most of our time during the yatra, in meditation and not in needless conversation. This way we could conserve our energies for the 'parikrama'. He also explained the import of both Manasarovar and Mt. Kailash. Manasarovar, the source of both the River Sindhu and the River Brahmaputra, washes the feet of Shiva and Shakti who reside beside the Lake in the form of Mt. Kailash. According to Kriya yoga, he said, the head symbolizes the Kailash and the heart, Manasarovar. Although the entire terrain has countless mountains, the attribution of sacredness only to Mt. Kailash indicates some mysterious sanctity. Sri M ended the satsang by telling us to 'keep a happy frame of mind' throughout the yatra.

When we came out of the dorm after satsang, cold breeze had begun to blow. Hot tomato soup and fresh popcorn came our way as the saving grace! This was followed by dinner, and of course, diamox. We chatted up for some time in our dorms and retired. Next morning we had to leave the place at 6 for Saga, our next destination.

DAY 5:

The day began at 5 am. It was still dark. After tea we were told to get into our vehicles parked in two rows outside the mud house complexes. Each of us was given packed breakfast. Our drivers were thoughtful enough to find their passengers and show them to their cars.

At 6, we left Nyalam. Most of us were still dozy but were not prepared to forego the distinct, spectacular beauty of the Tibetan Plateau. Our drivers were constantly praying and mumbling '*Om Manipamme Huum*' and other Tibetan chants. We later observed that not a single day of the yatra would begin without these prayers.

The roads were exceptional! A couple of our friends who were visiting Mt. Kailash in this route for the second time made us realize how lucky we were to have trimly laid roads now, which were but patchy and bumpy till two years ago. The morning glory in the land of mountains was a spectacle to delight in! As we drove higher in the Tibetan Plateau, vegetation grew sparse. The landscape reminded many of us of the mountains in the classic film 'Mackenna's Gold'. Some wild-life enthusiasts of the group spotted the occasional deer, a solitary emu or wild-ass en route.

Around 9.30 am our convoy reached the Lhapungla Pass at a height of about 16,000 ft. Two stone pillars stood on either side of the road and strung between them were Tibetan prayer flags with shredded white cloth. Every time our driver Patto spotted these flags, he would loudly utter '*so so so so so*' in a peculiar intonation. We found out that it meant 'best of luck' in Tibetan. Consequently, at the sight of these prayer flags thereafter, we joined him in the chants. In natural delight he would look at us, grin and shake his head in an approving nod. He would then say something in Tibetan and cackle heartily. We too laughed with him although we couldn't grasp a single sound of what he uttered.

Till then we were warm in our vehicles. When we got out of them at Lhapungla Pass, in a minute, we began to shiver in spite of our warm clothes. Sri M preferred to sit in the car. Some of our friends went to his window, chatted and had a sweet time with him.

It was foggy all over but afar, the snow-capped mountains glistened in soft sunlight! We were basking in that dreamy beauty when we were ushered back into our vehicles with shouts of *chalo chalo chalo*. Our drivers, who stopped and started whenever and wherever they wished to, had all together willed to start now!

The convoy hit the road again. We were now driving down to about 13,500 feet. Yet, some of us were gradually developing altitude sickness in the form of fever, nausea, headache, diarrhea, and constipation.

As far as the eyes could reach one could see but barren land, sand dunes, and layers of brown, black, and white peaks on both sides of the road. Fine dust sneaked into the closed vehicles. The dust mask that we wore throughout the travel filtered it to some extent. We moved on and on, and as if from nowhere a river with a noticeably large town on its banks suddenly came into view. It was Saga on the banks of the Brahmaputra! Till recently, it seems, people were ferried across to Saga by a launch on the river. Now there was an overpass through which we entered the town of Saga. When we got down at a characteristic modern lodge it was already two in the afternoon. The high altitude was indeed playing mischief, as a simple three storey climb to check into our rooms made us puff and pant.

Lunch was served by our Sherpas at 3 but some of us were hardly in a position to eat and digest anything spicy. Fresh fruits that were available just across the road came to rescue. It was announced that hot water would be provided between 8 pm and 12 pm and again for three hours in the morning. We would be having bath after three days. Not many of us ventured out of the rooms as we were exhausted due to lack of oxygen. By night the condition of some yatris turned worse and had us all worried. The doctor in our group, with assistants, kept checking the oxy-level of every one and administered apt medication to those with infirmity. Fatigue, anxiety and dilemma were written large on some faces during dinner time. Apparently as a fleeting consolation, Sri M said, "All will be well in one or two days."

The night was trying for both the doctor and the ailing friends. For many of us, the memory of Saga during the onward journey is that of 'a saga of discomfort'.

DAY 6:

An auspicious day! It was Gurupoornima and Sri M was with us. Everyone went to his room and sought blessings. And Manasarovar was just a day away!

The journey in the plateau continued as we left Saga at 10 in the morning after breakfast, for Prayang. The landscape was a mosaic of bald mountains, sand dunes, lakes and green pastures. Dawa Sherpa, one of our cooks, who traveled in our vehicle that day, informed us that the towering mountain that was visible in the distance was Sema Bangma, the fourth tallest in the world. Of the several lakes we passed, he showed one called Zhompa, that was world's second largest. Dawa seemed to have trekked in the terrain for numerous times to know the topography of the area so well.

On the verandah of a mud house complex in a dusty and arid village on the way, we were served lunch by the Sherpas. Perhaps due to the effect of diamox, our bodily ailments, and constant travel, no one could eat much. Anyway, sitting in a row along with Sri M on a verandah in an exotic and strange place to have lunch, was an experience by itself.

After an additional three hour journey, we pulled into another dusty town with bare (without plaster or paint) mud structures built up to a moderate height. Our vehicles were parked in a quadrangular enclosure with tall gates, with the name 'Payang Hotel' written on its wall.

After checking into our mud rooms and resting for sometime, we came out for tea. A satsang was planned in the courtyard within the quadrangle. In front of the platform where Sri M would be seated, a '*dhuni*' was lit. Sri M looked very special that evening in a *phiran*, the traditional Kashmiri robe.

He began the satsang by describing the intimate relationship of love and affection that a '*guru*' and a '*shishya*' shared. Narrating a few touching anecdotes from the years he spent with Babaji, his Master, he made us reflect upon the fact that the bond between a true guru and an earnest shishya is the rarest of all bonds.

When we are in the holy vicinity of the Manasarovar, he said, everyone must make time to sit and meditate. The low level of oxygen in the atmosphere at such high altitude may be an irritant to the body but is conducive to stimulate the psychic centres of the brain. As the message for Gurupoornima, he exhorted each of us to "keep the jewel in the lotus of the heart clean and pure," and not to hate anybody. After this unforgettable satsang, Sri M distributed some dry fruits as '*prasad*'. The full moon had begun to radiate resplendently. As we watched, we drifted into a mood of gratitude and contemplation.

Sri M had light dinner. Right from Nyalam he had been eating frugally. He kept asking all of us too to stay light. Those of us who were upset in health felt much well in Prayang, so much so, that a few of us went around actively clicking pictures.

Everywhere except in Saga, the major problem was the washroom facility and the toilet. All that existed were some pits and of course, nature! In Prayang we were cautioned not to venture out in the dark as there were wolf-like dogs on the prowl. We were left with no option but to use the two pits in a corner of the quadrangle. Besides, there was no water. Wet tissues were the only help. By then, however, we had quite got accustomed to this weird arrangement!

DAY 7:

Like the Tibetan nomads we met occasionally on the way, we too moved from place to place each day. If they moved in a horse carriage, we traveled by land rovers; that was the difference. Leaving Prayang at 9 in the morning after breakfast, we sped towards Manasarovar through more mountains, meadows, and lakes. The repetition of the landscape never became monotony. In reality, these 'inanimate' formations of the earth felt alive and familiar.

The convoy was stopped near a stream where there was a police check-post. The permit of the drivers was scrutinized by the Chinese police. We hardly missed any such opportunity to get out of our vehicles and take in the fresh air. Sri M too got out here and sauntered awhile. Noticing some of us who felt sick till Prayang now frisk around, he laughingly said, "It is good to finish off all the discomfort in the early days of the yatra rather than having them later."

Further ahead, we stopped near a tent-motel and a tent-shop. We wondered who their customers were; perhaps it was the yatris, drivers, and nomads as there were no settlements of any kind in the vicinity. Our sherpa-cooks spread the lunch table on the wayside plain near the motel! It was a splendid experience to eat rice, *channa*, *aloo* and *parwal*, pickle, and *rasgulla* on the plains, at the foothills of the ever charming mountain range. By this time, as Sri M had predicted, most of us were feeling fit.

At the end of an apparently endless drive, we caught sight finally of Manasarovar on our left at 3.30 in the afternoon! The blue sheet of water was a picture of peace. The magnificence of the Lake was enhanced by the backdrop of black hills shadowed by the clouds. A few seconds later, we beheld Mt. Kailash just above the right banks of the Lake.

Everyone stood spellbound, unable to believe that we were finally there! The harmony and quietude of the place moved our hearts so deeply that our hands folded instinctively and tears welled up in the eyes. Sri M's eyes were damp too though his face was sober as ever. He prostrated before Mt. Kailash and we touched his feet acknowledging to ourselves that we were here only by his grace.

Some of us wished to take a dip in Manasarovar and had to make our way to shallow waters. Once there we proceeded to enter the water and found it to be extremely cold while the sun was scorching hot. We could stay in the water for not more than a few minutes but that short dip was incredibly refreshing. In the next day's satsang, Sri M remembered how the little aches in his body vanished after the dip. On request Sri M sanctified the *rudraksha*s and *sphatika mala*s that many in the group wore, by immersing them in the holy Lake, and blessing them.

In no time, our clothes dried and we headed to the neighbouring lake, Rakshas Tal. Turquoise and still, it was a divine sight. As we watched, it turned sapphire and then azure and then back to turquoise. Both the Lakes have the distinct feature of changing hues in tune with the movement of clouds and the reflection of the mountains.

Meanwhile, the vehicle carrying Sri M went missing. After some enquiry and conjecture, we found out that it had broken down. When he finally arrived at the Jiumel Hotel on the opposite bank of Manasarovar, he responded coolly to our anxiety and disapproval about a snag in 'his' vehicle by saying, "Why? It's good that it happened to my vehicle than to anybody else's."

On most of the days after Katmandu, we had to manage with the things in our backpack—medicines, short eats, toiletries, and an extra pair of clothes. Our cargo bags used to follow us in a truck but were unloaded for us only in a place or two. We didn't need them though, as we couldn't take bath anywhere after Saga. We didn't even feel like, for we just couldn't imagine taking off the multiple layers of clothes we had piled on our body.

That evening was spent relaxing and enjoying the generous helpings of hot orange juice served by the cheery cooks! The gorgeous moon rose up in the sky right above the still glassy waters of the Lake.

Around two thirty in the morning some of us woke up and sat by the water for an hour or so. Time seemed to have come to a halt. Everything was still and tranquil.

DAY 8:

We would be staying at Manasarovar till that afternoon. The group gathered for a satsang at 10 in the morning, on the verandah outside Sri M's room.

Sri M spoke about the aches and pains that most of us felt during the journey. He told us that as long as the physical body existed this discomfort would be fairly common. He spoke of the complacency that all of us, living in luxury and convenience, possess and our blindness to simplicity and hardship of common life. The pilgrimage, he said, should reflect on the travails in our day to day life. He added that this pilgrimage should not end with the return to the plains since there is a larger pilgrimage ahead of us, that of life.

Sri M compared Mt. Kailash, a manifestation of Mahadeva, to the Truth. It is something that eyes cannot reach, words cannot describe, descriptions cannot encapsulate. It is something our mind cannot conceive of. We were on a pilgrimage to that eternal, unutterable, inexplicable and indescribable Truth.

Sri M equated the pilgrimage to our daily life; we do not know where we are going or what we are going to face. Yet we fare on consistently to find the Truth. The head is the Kailash where Mahadeva resides, and the body symbolizes the trees, water, mountains and other features. He told us that when one does the parikrama, one must remember that one is paying homage to the Mahadeva in one's head and understand that one is not a mere bundle of flesh and bones.

This satsang helped us embark on the parikrama with the right perspective. At the end of Sri M's talk, our Nepalese tour manager Tarkei briefed us as to how the parikrama has to be undertaken. He advised us that each one should be on one's own, and walk at individual pace, not competing with anyone else. He suggested that we walk slowly and steadily and practice reticence to conserve oxygen and energy. He told us clearly that this was a personal journey and even the spouses need not stick together.

Following this we visited Cho Ghompa (water monastery) situated on a hillock about a kilometer and a half in the direction opposite to the Lake. A lone Buddhist priest was chanting his regular morning prayers. It seemed that he had just then offered dry fish, meat and liquor to the Buddha!

After lunch we left the place for Darchen. It was a one and a half hour drive. Darchen is the base camp for the trek to Mt.Kailash. The hotel in which we were to stay, seemingly clean and modern from outside, turned out to be the lousiest and the filthiest accommodation we were to have in the entire journey. Unfortunately there was nowhere else to stay because the town of Darchen was but two roads in a right angle with absolutely no accommodation other than the hotel we had checked into. To add to our woes, another batch of yatris was staying in the same hotel making everything very cramped and crowded. A few Tibetan women vendors made the most of this. They went around selling some attractive bead-chains hung on their forearm for display.

As we stood wondering how to occupy the stinking rooms, Sri M settled in his with characteristic nonchalance and said, "It's okay. Anyway we are going to spend only a night here." This gave us confidence and strength to ignore the unpleasant odour. We lit plenty of incense sticks, sprayed perfumes and deodorants to make the rooms as habitable as possible. With the door kept open for long the air gradually turned bearable.

We were asked to repack our backpacks to keep them within 15 kgs. Any additional weight would be charged for by the porters. Soon the tour coordinators went around and took bookings for ponies or porters or both according to our needs. While only some chose to take ponies, we were advised that everyone should hire porters as even the strongest members would find it impossible to do the trek carrying backpacks.

Sri M was in the same buoyant mood that had kept us afloat through these seven days during which we 'ate, drank, talked, joked, meditated, laughed and travelled'.

After dinner we retired early, anticipating favourable climate the next day.

DAY 9:

The morning was sunny and warm which was a good sign for us yatris. The distant mountain peaks, however, were misty and obscured but rains didn't seem to be in the offing. At around ten we got into our respective land cruisers and left for Yamadwar, the symbolic gateway to Mt. Kailash. We were lucky to catch a rare glimpse of Mt. Kailash from Yamadwar. We lingered in the place for some time taking pictures, and paying obeisance to Mahadeva and Sri M. A little ahead of Yamadwar we got out of our vehicles and waited to be allotted ponies and porters for the parikrama. We sat waiting for the allotment, at the foothills of Kailash. Noticing that there was a shortage of ponies and porters (nearly two hundred yatris were preparing for the parikrama on that single day), some of us began to eat our packed lunch that consisted of an apple, biscuits, chocolate, and juice.

At last, after a wait of one and a half hour, registered men and women porters, with their name and registration number written in a slip, were given to each of us. We handed over our rucksacks to these Tibetan porters who spoke and understood no other language but the Tibetan. We had to trust and entrust our things and personal safety to them.

By this time Sri M had already left with a Sherpa-cook who was allotted as his porter. As we waited for our porters, we caught sight of Sri M in the distance walking steadily, stick in hand with his Sherpa following him.

The groceries, gas cylinders, tent material etc were tied on a herd of yaks that would carry them for us and trek up to Derapuk where we would camp for the day. By two in the afternoon, one by one, we too began to tread along with our porter. The first day's walk was immensely enjoyable and not too tiring as we were walking mostly on the plains. We had the enthralling darshan of the southern, the western and the northern faces of Mt. Kailash on this very first day! During the trek we discovered that most of the porters were more than trustworthy although a few were negligent. Some of them were so caring and thoughtful that the moment your feet faltered and you slowed down, they held your water bottle in front of you and offered '*paani*', the only Hindi word they knew. On rocky paths and wobbly bridges they offered you a ready helping hand. At such times, we often found ourselves wondering whether it was Shiva or Shakti coming to our aid in the form of porters!

A little while later, we spotted Sri M sitting alone on a boulder, resting for a while. We were simply delighted to join him and had the good fortune of walking with him for the rest of the day. All through the trek, the river Dera kept flowing beside us in the opposite direction. Around 6.30 pm we reached Derapuk, a plain land with mounds and a row of mud houses. The mud houses were occupied by another group of yatris. Further away, at the base of the northern face of Mt. Kailash, our Sherpa-cooks had begun pitching our tents. Even though we had started at the same time, the Sherpa-cooks had reached much earlier and we were amazed at their physical endurance and mental disposition. First of all they pitched a tent for Sri M, and then for the kitchen. Suddenly before all the tents were up it began to rain. Those of us who had reached the camp site took shelter in the kitchen tent. One or two friends who were still on the way were drenched by the time they reached despite having their raincoats on. Meanwhile, our tour coordinators and some considerate youngsters in the group had swung into action by joining hands with the Sherpas in pitching tents for all.

It rained for quite long even after we occupied the twin sharing tents. During all this while, fortunately daylight lingered; the sunset occurs only at around 9 pm in that part of China. At around 10 when darkness fell at last the rain stopped and we crawled out of the tents with flash lights. The amazing Sherpas had already made soup, *papad* and *khichdi* for dinner. Before dinner the doctor couple checked our oxygen levels. This entire time Sri M stayed in the tent and hadn't come out after entering it in the evening. Food was served to him in his tent.

Sleep didn't come easily that night although we were exhausted. We were in a kind of stupor, unable to believe that we were indeed sleeping in the lap of Lord Mahadeva! After a while, however, this blissful musing lulled our tired body and content mind to an uninterrupted sleep.

DAY 10:

This was to be the most demanding day of the yatra. The Sherpa-cooks were up by 5 am and were making tea. At 6 two of them went around the tents serving piping hot bed tea to all. One of them kept calling out near every tent, "*Garam garam mousam mein thanda thanda chai…*" (cold, cold tea in hot, hot weather…) and smiled, amused by his own sense of humour.

The day break was spectacular with the first rays of the sun making one of the peaks visible from the camp appear as if it was ablaze! Mt.Kailash, however, was still covered with a light film of fog. At this point, some of the yatris decided against proceeding with the Parikrama and were sent back to Darchen, after consulting Sri M, accompanied by a Sherpa.

The day was expected to be the most trying of the three days of the parikrama. We were to trek for 23 kilometers and reach our next camp site, Zuthulpuk. We started at 8.30 am after a light breakfast of corn flakes with sugar or honey, and milk. At an altitude of 17,000 ft, in the chill weather one didn't feel like eating more. Also, we had to walk; to eat something heavy would become a disadvantage.

The ponies, yaks, and the porters who had camped near the Dera River, joined us in the morning for the day's walk. A few of us got the opportunity to keep pace with Sri M like the previous day. He walked at a moderate pace, stopping for a minute or two every time he saw us tired. We took these breaks as opportunities to wonder silently at the beauty around us, and observe everything, animate and inanimate including oneself, silently engaged in the task of the moment. With minimum talk, everyone, the members of ours as well as of other groups, focused intensely on each step that they took. There was, in reality, no group. All were one, yet each was independent.

You couldn't entirely rely upon your porters because unable to hold back their pace to match with ours they would, once in a while, walk ahead of us, and relaxing on a boulder at a point, wait for us. A middle-aged lady porter held a *japamala* in her hand and constantly muttered '*Om Manipamme Huum*'. We too chanted in the mind '*Om Hrim Namah Shivaya*' which Sri M had asked us to do while on the parikrama.

There was no definite path anywhere. We just kept walking one behind the other, making way now and then, for ponies and yaks. After the first two hours we were breathless from the lack of oxygen in the air. We tried dog breathing to rejuvenate the lungs. We popped sugar candies and other sweets from our waist pouch which energized us instantly.

Throughout one heard but the wind, the Tibetan care takers of the animals holler at them when sometimes they halted and refused to budge, and the clink of the bells around the yaks' neck. Only when we stopped to rest could we look up and around. Otherwise, our attention was firmly set on the rocky, dangerous path that stretched for miles. In such a terrain, being on a pony was all the more scary. We witnessed a few pony riding yatris fall off them with a thud. What ensued was a blame game between the rider and the Tibetan pony man.

None of us knew how long the walk would last. Since our paces differed the only aim was to reach Zuthulpuk, wherever it was, before that night. It was noon. Our packed lunch (apple, juice, biscuits etc) was in the knapsack but we decided against eating to stay light. However, we often took sips of water to retain the oxygen levels in the body. A gorge was sighted in the distance and people in it like ants in file! This gorge was the Dolmala Pass we were meant to cross. It was an intimidating prospect but Sri M cautioned us not to think of the destination but take the immediate step carefully. Heeding to his advice, we continued with renewed vigour. We gradually began to befriend the hostile territory. Two hours later, we were walking in the same stretch that we had dreaded from a distance! By 2.30 in the afternoon, we were at the highest point of our walk in the parikrama, the Dolmala Pass at a height of 18,600 ft. The spot was a field of fluttering prayer flags offered at the rustic stone shrine of Dolmala Devi. As per instruction we were not to stay at the spot for more than a few minutes because of the lowest oxy level in the air. After a quick break we stood on our feet again to progress.

A group of Tibetan yatris were doing the '*kora*' (Tibetan for '*parikrama*') anti-clockwise, while we walked clockwise. Also they did it by prostrating at every step around Kang Rinpoche (Mt. Kailash)! They wore padded palm and knee guards to avoid getting bruised by the incessant prostration. The porters sometimes cleared the stone ridden narrow paths to help out both the Hindu and the Buddhist yatris.

From the Dolmala Pass, we had to descend, which was as strenuous as the ascent, if not more. Our walking sticks were our guardians during the down hill climb. All those on the ponies had to now dismount and continue on foot. The ponies were not employed to take the yatris down as the path was slippery and narrow. Nevertheless the pony men took their ponies down and waited for their yatris near a tent motel that was at the end of the descent.

The climate so far was congenial to our expedition. On the way we caught a glimpse of Gauri Kund, a small pond, in the middle of a chasm. Mahadeva's consort Gauri is believed to take bath in the pond. Sri M sent his Sherpa-porter to fetch the holy water of the Kund to be distributed as '*teertha*' to the group. The Sherpa ran down and came up with the water filled bottle, in no time!

Finally we saw a large tent down in the plains. The tent motel! We were close to finishing the feat, we thought. Walking in the plains could be easier after what we had accomplished. We sat outside the motel to relax. Someone bought a cup of Chinese noodle soup for Sri M. Some others ate what was in their backpack. After a pretty long respite, we hit the track again. The pony yatris were back on their ponies.

The weather was now erratic. If warm clothes were removed because of perspiration a cold wind would suddenly rise forcing them back on. Forging ahead, our speed would suddenly be interrupted by freezing cold rain forcing us to wear raincoats. No shelter could be sought as the terrain was all barren and open with no vegetation whatsoever.

We walked for over three hours in these plains. It was already six in the evening. The sun continued to work. Soon we could sense the end of our walk. Sri M's porter, pointing beyond a hillock ahead, assured us that our camp was close. Saying this he walked past us swiftly as he and his co-workers had to pitch tents for the group.

Nevertheless, the path seemed everlasting. "I can feel every part of my body," said one yatri while another disagreed and said, "I can't feel any part of my body; everything's numb." We were disoriented by ten hours of grueling, incessant walk. As if to draw us back to the world around, there formed a charming rainbow between two mountains! The sun and the drizzle had gifted it to us.

There! We spotted some tents far away. As we walked closer we realized that they were not ours. Ours were red and orange ones; those were blue and green. What a disappointment! Walking further became excruciating, yet inevitable. Our backs were cracking. We literally followed our involuntary footsteps. But Sri M continued to walk upright and unnerved. He kept persuading us to keep heart. There was an affectionate encouragement in his voice that saved us from giving in.

At last, we caught sight of 'our' tents. Some of our friends had already reached. Sri M's party reached by 7.30 in the evening. Many were still on their way. Concern that if darkness fell they would be disoriented grew amongst us but the Nepali team manager assured us that he would make sure every yatri reached safely. The last few yatris, and the Nepalese tour manager behind them, pulled in at 8.30! The tents were pitched and ready for occupation by then. Most of us simply collapsed on the foam mattresses in our tents, trying to straighten the back. A heartfelt gratitude was mentally offered to Sri M for helping us complete the trial! Once he entered his tent, Sri M didn't appear at all, even during dinner.

It began to rain by 9. Rains seemed to be an every evening feature in the hills. By then our soup, *papad* and *khichdi* were ready. We deserved every morsel of food and every wink of sleep that night. After dinner we slept peacefully with an immeasurable sense of fulfillment in the mind.

DAY 11:

It was the third day of the parikrama. We awoke at 6 in high spirits. The biggest hurdle in the yatra had been successfully crossed. Friends who were not healthy in the early part of the journey had also completed the phenomenal task. We were overwhelmed by our own accomplishment and needless to say, we knew the source of the strength with which we had achieved this.

This day we had to walk a mere 8 kilometers! Like the earlier two days, after a light breakfast we commenced the walk. A few of us walked along with Sri M. We had walked up for barely ten minutes from the camp site, when we came upon a gurgling stream that needed to be crossed. The yatris on ponies were led straight through it while the rest had to inch across a loosely made bridge of logs and poles. The ponies walked across the stream with the rider on the back and climbed up the muddy path up to the elevation. At this point the pony man usually didn't accompany the rider but walked on the bridge.

As we were crossing the bridge we heard a loud groan. To our astonishment we saw that one of our friends had fallen off his pony right at the upper edge of the elevation! The muddy climb had become slippery and while climbing up, his pony slipped and he fell off on his back along with the saddle which perhaps was fastened loosely to the animal. The pony was equally stunned as the rider, and had run away. The owner of the pony was not to be seen as he had handed it over, with the rider, to his 10 to 12 year old son to mind! The boy too had escaped. There was no point in thinking of asking for an explanation from a man who wasn't there. Our friend, meanwhile, was writhing in pain. Apparently, his back was severely injured. Sri M stood right next to him and gestured to him not to be anxious. The doctor in the group hadn't reached the spot yet. One by one all of us gathered around him incredulously. Soon the doctor too arrived. After he checked him up by moving his limbs, it was decided that he should be carried. His situation appeared to be alarming as he could just not move. A stretcher was made using bed sheets, some wooden walking sticks, shoe laces, nylon ropes, and anything that came in handy. The entire group had assembled around him and was in no mood to continue the parikrama without our friend. Sri M suggested that apart from ten strong men who would help carry the injured person by turns, the rest should continue the trek. All the women and a few men left the spot praying for our friend's speedy recovery.

Despite this incident and some narrow stretches in between, the third day's walk was quite easy. This walk would conclude at a place little away from Manasarovar where our land rovers waited. The path was attractive, speckled with green pastures, indicating that we were walking down to the plains. A vast sheet of shimmering light shone at a distance. Manasarovar! It felt like homecoming to see it. By one in the afternoon we arrived at the spot where our land cruisers were parked. The vehicles that were dirty and dusty when we had left them before the parikrama, were all washed and had worn a new look. Our driver Patto came running, seeing us approach our vehicle. He smilingly offered a big bottle of water he had specially filled for us, and spiritedly said "Kang Rinpoche"! He seemed to be pleased with our successful completion of the parikrama.

After an hour or so, the party carrying the patient arrived. Sri M too had walked with them. The Sherpa-cooks reportedly played a major role in carrying our friend at some crucial narrow turns on the way. On their arrival the drivers immediately offered to help. The rear seat of one of the land rovers was folded and our friend placed down on it so he could complete the journey lying down. Two of our other friends accompanied him in the vehicle.

The convoy then headed to the camp site in Manasarovar. On reaching there, after serving us packed lunch comprising *jeera* rice, *channa* and white rice, the Sherpas pitched our tents on the bank of Manasarovar. Sri M entered his tent for a nap and did not come into sight until the next morning.

The evening was a memorable one in many ways. The day was so sunny that some elders in the group advised youngsters not to expose themselves to sunlight and wind all at once by removing the warm clothes. Already many of our faces had tanned, some had bloated a little, and the eyes seemed to have shrunk! Each of our bodies had reacted differently to the mixed climate of the region.

Friends who could not take a dip in the Manasarovar during the onward journey went for it now. Some others went for a second dip. Some more happily basked in the sun outside their tents. Everybody was feeling fit and cheerful. Those who had returned to Darchen half way from the parikrama joined us here with their caretaker Sherpa.

From this bank of Manasarovar we could get a clear view of the snow-capped mountain Gurla Mandata on the left, and a hazy view of Mt. Kailash right in front. As we enjoyed the sun and the scenic beauty around, dusk fell. The sunset painted myriad hues in the sky offering a feast to the eyes. In the meantime, a loud cheer hit our ears from the dining tent (was pitched only here). There were hot French fries and mixed vegetable soup as starters for dinner! A few teenagers in the group had, from the previous day, been craving for French fries. They couldn't believe that prayers could be answered that shortly and to that extent! They hugged each other, hooted, and raised their thumbs unable to contain their elation.

Meanwhile, our friend who had fallen off his pony (Sri M later changed it as 'the pony that fell off his back') was on his feet! He could not bend or walk swiftly but was less reliant. We were relieved to see him as his usual laughing self.

That was a happy night. Our greatest mission in life was accomplished! All anxieties and apprehensions had vanished. From the next morning we would begin our journey back home.

Manasarovar to Katmandu: The return journey was precisely in the same route as the onward one. Free from all qualms and expectations we made the most of our powers of observation to take in the sights of this part of Tibet. Though beautiful, we noticed that it was terribly impoverished and backward. The life of the Tibetans here was dismal. They lived merely as wage workers, as small time vendors or as road makers.

By the time we reached Prayang our bodies had turned sticky with grime. It was already eight days since we had a shower! As soon as we reached the mud houses in Prayang we tried to wash, at least, our hands and face with just one mug of water. Everyone was in a gay mood, but looked forward to go to Saga where we could have a refreshing bath.

Next day, on the way to Saga, when we had stopped to have packed lunch near the tent motel, our drivers squatted in a circle on the grass for a banquet! Two Tibetan women of the tent motel brought big chunks of yak meat in a carton, some *roti*s, and salt tea etc placed them amidst the voracious drivers. They had a good time mocking one another and roaring with laughter. How oblivious they were to the people and the world around them!

By late afternoon we were in Saga. Sitting in the lobby of the hotel waiting for the allotment of rooms, everyone began to recollect the state of many of us in Saga just a few days ago. The past days appeared like a dream. Some of us had already started to yearn for home food. All were waiting to have a thorough bath from head to toe. Our German friend in the group went to the extent of saying 'If there is not enough water in the hotel,

I'll go buy all the water bottles in Saga town. If they are not sufficient, I'll buy beer for bath!' There were peals of laughter.

That evening all of us got busy in bringing our bodies back to normal. Sri M wore a neat look after a shave and a shower. We came out of our rooms for dinner looking clean and fresh. Moreover, the altitude of Saga that was so upsetting some days ago could do nothing to us now.

The journey back was indeed a jaunt. In between Saga and Nyalam, we stopped beside a stream for lunch. Our drivers were in their usual joyous mood. Most of them jumped into the water to have a wash, God knows after how many days! Many of us too took off our shoes and slipped our feet into the cool water. Sitting like this all together in a long row, we got our pictures clicked. The ladies wanted an all women's photograph with Sri M! He kindly obliged and posed with us.

We reached Nyalam late in the evening. One indeed lost the sense of time in this territory as the sun's clock didn't match with ours. In Nyalam we met a batch of Indian yatris from Spain who were on their way to Mt. Kailash. They were just as anxious as we were some days before, about how things would turn out for them. They had a hundred queries which some of us tried to answer, in order to boost up their morale, knowing fully well that any amount of caution and precaution about this yatra didn't actually matter unless one was destined to complete it.

After a night in Nyalam, we left for Katmandu at 6 in the morning, when it was still dark. Though the distance was not much, we had decided to start early in order to reach Kodari before 10 O' clock, so that the immigration process could get over by noon. It turned out to be a reasonable decision. In an hour after we set out, all our vehicles came to a standstill due to a heavy landslide on a narrow path. In the darkness we couldn't accurately perceive the magnitude of the landslide. It must have been quite heavy, we guessed, seeing the number of vehicles that were held up on either side of it. There was nothing that could be done except wait till help came. The drivers seemed to be least troubled by this as it was only common to them in these mountain roads.

At the crack of dawn some of us alighted from our vehicles to inspect the landslide. We saw that it was massive. Besides, a giant road roller was left in the middle of the road, probably by the workers when they had stopped work the previous evening. After a long hour, a troupe of Chinese officers and Tibetan workers arrived and made efforts to clear the road. Around 8 we started again and reached Kodari at 10, perfectly on time and as per our plan. After the passport and baggage check at the Immigration Bureau we walked across the Friendship Bridge to Nepal. On the other side of the bridge three buses were waiting to take us to Katmandu. Around 12.30 noon we were driven to a refreshing rive-side restaurant. After a stroll in the landscaped restaurant and a sumptuous meal we headed to Katmandu.

On our return on 16th July, we were put up at Hotel Royal Singi in Katmandu. The whole evening was spent in walking up and down the streets. The hotel offered a grand dinner that night.

On 17th July, the last day of our yatra, we gathered in the hotel for a farewell satsang. It was in this satsang that Sri M revealed the reason for his staying a majority of the time in his tent and for mingling the least with the group during the parikrama days. He told us that "something else was functioning (in me) of the good old days."

Sri M modestly thanked everyone in the group for direct or indirect help in making the yatra a successful one. He thanked the tour operators Sri Sudhakar, Sri Ratnakar and Sri Jayaprakash who traveled with us throughout and cared for our comforts.

That afternoon we had to leave Katmandu for home. The sense of fulfillment that welled up in every yatri's heart was palpable. Everybody embarked on a journey back home with a heavy heart as we had to get back to the rut of mundane life. However, the life we reverted to was not to be the same as before. We hoped to live it with a better understanding, after the yatra to Mt. Kailash. For, as Sri M said, the parikrama was not complete yet; it was to be continued in our everyday life with the same fervour and equanimity as one adopted during the parikrama to Kailash. We had indeed been introduced to a novel dimension of perceiving life. With the end of the yatra to Mt. Kailash, we looked forward to the dawn of a newer insight into life and the way we were to live it.

A towering idol of Buddha at Baudhanath temple, Kathmandu

Consider this pilgrimage
to Kailash
to be the same as our life's journey
towards the lofty heights of Truth.
Mahadeva represents that Truth.
When you go on this pilgrimage, reflect
on this matter,
that in everyday life too we are
on a pilgrimage.

– Sri M

Kailash-Manasarovar Yatra

Satsang with Sri M

Magenta Press

Other titles by Sri M

- Shunya - A Novel
- On Meditation
- The Home Coming & Other Stories
- Yoga also for the Godless
- Apprenticed to a Himalayan Master A Yogi's Autobiography
- The Little Guide to Greater Glory and a Happier Life
- Wisdom of the Rishis
  Ishavasya, Kena, Mandukya
- Jewel in the Lotus
  Deeper Aspects of Hinduism
- How to Levitate and other Great Secrets of Magic
  by James Talbot (Sri M)
- The Upanishads
  Katha, Prashna, Mundaka
- The Journey Continues
  Sequel to Apprenticed to a Himalayan Master

Translations available of Sri M's autobiography:

- Hindi
- Telugu
- Bengali
- Spanish
- Marathi
- Malayalam
- Tamil
- Japanese
- Oriya
- Kannada
- Gujarati
- German
- Russian
- Italian

To buy books, DVD's and Digital downloads online visit www.magentapress.in

KAILASH-MANASAROVAR YATRA

Satsang at Nyalam

We've gathered here for a brief satsang on the way to Mount Kailash. There are different ways of going to Mount Kailash: You can trek, you can go mountaineering, you can go as a tourist. So we should work out between ourselves what is our attitude of going to Mount Kailash. If you consider Mount Kailash as merely a mountain it is there, merely as a mountain: you go around and come back. If you consider it as a place where since ancient times, people have been going on pilgrimage, and if you don't want to consider all these people, who have been going on pilgrimage for thousands and hundreds of years as fools, then you can go with the understanding that there might be something more than just a mountain out there. I'm not saying that I have seen Shiva sitting there with Parvati or anything of the kind. I don't know, because I haven't seen, because I haven't been to Kailash, and nobody usually climbs to the top of Kailash. So we don't know what the situation up there is. We can only go in a helicopter and take a photograph of the top. We don't know if mountaineers have gone; I have no idea.

What I want to say is that certain sacredness is attached to these places, Manasarovar and Mount Kailash for hundreds of years. In the Puranas the story is that Krishna took the

Pandavas to Mount Kailash along the river Saraswati from Badrinath, and according to the Mahabharat, Mahadeva himself came to welcome them, fed them and sent them back. Unfortunately, my first attempt at going to Mount Kailash ended up in a little bit of a disaster, so I had to come back half way. I am talking of 1969. However, then I did not go this way. There is another path, which is very interesting but I don't think we can go that way now, because there isn't any cut out path over there.

In 1969, after I met my master, may be two weeks after I met him, I expressed a desire to go see a place called Tholing Mutt. It is an ancient Buddhist temple with the Buddha so high that it touches the roof. I had heard from a Tibetan wandering yogi that there are certain things to be seen in Tholing Mutt. Actually at the back of my mind I also had this secret desire to see a *yeti*, a snowman. I wanted to go to that monastery and spend some time, so I expressed the desire to Babaji. He said, 'If you walk another four days you will reach Kailash but that is not this direction. You will go to Kailash first and then you will come to Manasarovar from the other direction.' So we set out one day, one early morning, with a yak provided by Ravalji of Badrinath. You know Badrinath has these Namboodiri priests. There one Mr. Keshava Namboodiripad provided a yak for us, and some merchants. Marvaris, who were known to Babaji provided a Sherpa, a Nepalese man called Fateh Bahadur, who would take the yak and also cook for us. So, with this guy, one tent and provisions on the yak we set out. I was of course properly padded up with warm clothes

and wearing canvas shoes but Babaji as usual, was bare bodied, wearing a small cotton cloth around his waist and a rolled up blanket on the back, with an axe fixed on it, to be used to cut firewood to make the *dhuni* in the evenings.

Off we went. We had to halt in the night, only in the tent because there was no other place to halt. It took us exactly 13 days to reach the top of the Mana Pass—it is 18,600 feet above sea level. By then I had such a severe headache and nausea that I was wondering whether this was a foolhardy thing to do, to come on this trip. The food was okay: this man used to make chapattis and alu and we had enough kerosene and a hurricane lamp in the tent. All three of us slept in the tent. It would be wrong to say three of us slept in the tent, two of us slept, because I have never seen Babaji sleep. While we fell asleep, he would be sitting near the *dhuni*. My last vision of him, before sleeping, would always be of him sitting like this, not meditating with eyes open. So we walked and climbed up the Pass: that side of the Pass is Tibet, this side of the Pass is India.

We climbed down. Once you climb down, the whole terrain changes: there are grasslands, the earth is red, there are plains, flat plains. The mountains are on either side, on which you can see ice, faraway. So when I went there I said, 'Ah! This is fine, now we are definitely going to Tholingmutt.' In three days we reached Tholingmutt. By then I had a slight temperature—I ignored it. We spent three days in Tholingmutt with the Rinpoche there. Babaji was having some discussions with him. I also had some questions which I now think were pretty stupid

questions. In those days I thought they were very serious ones. We had a discussion; good food was provided to us. Babaji's food was specially cooked but He never ate. I was enjoying myself. Then when the fever started, they began to give me some Tibetan medicines. The next stop was a place called Dhaba. Dhaba was already a marketplace—there was a big monastery and lots of monks. We met the head of the monastery. At the *Avalokiteshvara's* temple we spent some time.

The next stop was supposed to be Mandi, which was a very big market place. In olden days people from India would go from Almora side; silk merchants came from China. Spices and various other things were sold. At Dhaba I fell so ill, that I became delirious. I started getting convulsions. The *lamas* requested Babaji to shift me. He refused. He gave me a wooden cot to lie down upon but the fever did not subside. They tried all kinds of Tibetan medicine. While the delirium continued, one night I woke up, sweating profusely and something happened, which I don't want to reveal to you. I saw something weird. When I told Babaji the next day about what I thought it was, He said, 'Don't tell anybody, they will just think you were delirious, so just shut up!' Then from there he said we can't go to Kailash. It was only four days more to go to Kailash. He said, 'Wapas chalo, mar jaoge' (go back, otherwise you will die). So I was literally put on the yak and kind of bound on it and for half the way I was like that and they brought me down. In nine days we reached Badrinath. After about five days I recovered. A week after I convalesced I said, 'Babaji phir chalte hain' (we will

go to Kailash again). He told me something very interesting. He said, 'Abhi nahin jaoge, bahut saal baad jaoge' (you will not go now, you will go after many years). 'Bahut log saath honge tumhare' (many people will be with you). I got really frightened, I said 'Kyon? Bahut log kyon aayenge, akela jana hai.' (Why many people? I want to go alone). He said, 'Nahin nahin, abhi kuch nahin samjhoge, baad mein samajh ayega' (you will not understand now, you will understand later).

By the way he said I couldn't ask him anything else. I kept quiet. It is very funny that for years the thought of going to Kailash did not occur to me. Only for the last two years I have been thinking about it. Last year, when I expressed it, everybody got into this. So I think about what Babaji said, I am going with so many people.

Therefore for me, this trip is a very, very important trip. Since I am also writing my autobiography, this will probably be my last chapter. After this, I will not write anything. So, if it is so important, there must be some reason why one would take so much trouble and go up the mountain.

First thing is, it is through pilgrimages like this, difficult pilgrimages... This is really not difficult, we have rooms to stay, we have woollen clothes to wear, we have cars to take us. This is not the way I used to wander around. It used to be so difficult. Sometimes you wouldn't have proper woollen clothes—you stayed in caves or in little places, wherever available. In the night, sometimes you woke up thinking you are going to die and called Babaji who was sitting near the fire at

night. We are actually in real comfort, think of that. Whenever you are faced with any difficulty, think that we are in so much comfort. We are not really wandering like that, and yet, we have a desire to go. There are difficulties, our difficulties are nothing compared to the difficulties that *sadhus* face. For example, I'll tell you: We know about Badri, we know about Kedar. People go to Kedarnath, because many people come there, it is well known. Everybody goes there; but between Badrinath and Kedarnath—in the Chaukhamba range there are small other '*naths*'. You have Mudh-Maheshwar on the top, you have Tunganath on this side, you have Rudranath, and you have Kalpeshwar on that side. These are not pilgrim routes. Few people go there. The only people there are some *sadhus* or some very adventurous travellers. These are beautiful places, out of this earth, but cold, with difficult-to-walk terrain. Sometimes you have to climb great heights, and then you descend. You have to stay probably in the temple. In Rudranath, there is hardly a temple; even in the temple complex, there is no image. So in such difficult places you wander—that is the real pilgrimage. Compared to that... That is why I am going around with a song on my lips because everything is so.... We may have some difficulties with the weather or with the oxygen but that is something beyond our control. The rest what we can control, we have them all. So consider that whenever you get into any difficulty, they are only small, minor things.

Probably on Guru Purnima, we will be in Manasarovar or Paryang. Now you are going nearer to Kailash, I just want to

tell you this: I don't want you to believe anything. Please sit down and meditate in these places and see if you feel a difference from meditating somewhere else, then you will yourself realize that there is something going on. Deliberately I do not want to define what is going on. These definitions then, spoil the sanctity of things.

There is Supreme Energy, which the moment you begin to describe and define, is gone. It is finished. If you don't know then we will work something out. Don't worry. Basically be one pointed and keep quiet, think. Does everybody know to meditate? You have been trying to do it, but…

What I suggest is that as we go along, whenever you get a calm feeling, whenever you get a situation where you can sit quietly, with me or without me—doesn't matter—sit quietly and do two things: either open your eyes and be fully merged with what you see—beautiful mountains, rivers, waterfalls and trees. This is the Manifest Supreme. Or, if you want to go into the inner side, what is inside you, close your eyes, fix your attention in your heart or in between your eyes and sit quietly. You are going to Kailash, and it is associated with Mahadeva. Mahadeva simply means the highest Deva.He need not necessarily be deified as Shankara, with a snake around his neck. '*Maha*' is a word used for something which cannot be explained, described or defined. Since Kailash is identified as the seat of Mahadeva, all you have to do is to close your eyes and chant the mantra of Mahadeva as you are going. That's it! The mantra is '*Om Namah Shivaya*'. Everybody knows it. It has been chanted everywhere. It is not a must to chant *Om Namah*

Shivaya. The true meaning of *Om Namah Shivaya* is '*shivohum*'. So sit quietly and see if you can identify Shiva inside you. If you can't identify Shiva inside you, identify Shiva with the great mountains. In fact, in Kedarnath there is a temple but, Kedarnath's majesty is in the ice clad peaks behind the temple. The temple is a symbol of that vastness. Either you worship that Supreme vastness, if you are of that bent inside you, or open your eyes and see the vastness as it is outside. At that time no unnecessary thoughts should be allowed to come into your mind. That's all is the function of chanting. If you don't want to think of Shiva, if you think you are a *Vaishnavite*, then simply say 'Om'. It is applicable everywhere.

So as we go along, right from tomorrow, or today, whenever you get a few moments, sit quietly and do this. Others who have been instructed in meditation, can follow whatever has been given or taught to them. If you want a simple way, just close your eyes, watch your breath as you breathe in and out. Give complete attention to your breathing. Inhalation, you take in, chant, think that it is one '*Om*' going in. When you breathe out, think that it is one '*Om*' coming out. Just keep that in mind and sit quietly. If you like the heart centre, if you are a person who constantly keeps falling in love, fix your attention in the heart center. If you think you are a very philosophical person, fix your attention between the eyes and sit quietly. Let the mind rest. Resting is the most important thing. Therefore, when you walk, when you are tired, in the night when you stop the day's work, automatically the body is so tired that it has to rest. Let the mind also rest. Sink all the

anxieties of tomorrow. 'What is going to happen tomorrow? Am I going to climb?' Let go of all the troubles of today and just sit quietly. That is what I mean by meditation. Fix your attention on the top of the mountain and bow down to Shiva. It's very difficult to say 'I am Shiva' so bow down to Shiva. When you begin to say 'I am Shiva' then quickly arrogance creeps into the mind.

Please tell us about the Rudrakasha.

The literal meaning of the word *Rudraksha* is Rudra's eyes. Since ancient times, in the areas around Gandaki River in Nepal, the *rudraksha* trees have been growing and sadhus since ancient times have used the *rudraksha* for chanting, as a rosary. Since it is a plant, sometimes naturally it has only one side, sometimes it has two sides, sometimes it has three sides but the most common and natural one is the five side. It is called '*panchamukhi*'. Now since one side and two sides are rare, they have been given more importance. Symbolically, because if it has two sides it is called '*Shiva Shakti*'. One sided one is called '*Ishwara*' and the '*panchamukhi*' is called '*panch tatwas*' and all that. These are all basically symbolic.

If you ask me if there is any special significance in your *sadhana* in wearing a *rudraksha*, I would say that the *rudraksha* has an effect in meditation since it is the eye of the Rudra, identified and symbolized as eye of Rudra. What is Rudra? Rudra means destroyer. So only very dedicated *sadhakas*, who don't mind the world crumbling and

still want to reach their goal, should play with *rudraksha*. Others should better restrict themselves to *tulasi* or *sphatika* or something like that. Great saints have had *rudrakshamalas* but they don't care what happens to the world. Since Mahadeva is associated with Kailash and since Manasarovar is supposed to be washing his feet, *rudraksha* dipped in Manasarovar is considered holy, because it is like *abhisheka*—similar to going to a temple and pouring water over the *Linga*. Shiva as a deity, is the manifestation of the Supreme Energy, and is the simplest deity to worship. He does not want anything. You can offer one *bilvapatra* and pour some water, which is all that is required. Now pouring water means cleaning. You will see where there are *Shivalingas* and when you can't do daily puja, people just hang a pot with a small hole in it and fill it with water. It keeps dripping. All over India you will find this—so simple! Therefore, water has become so important for the worship of a *Shivalinga*. Therefore, Manasarovar is important because it is doing constant *abhisheka* and it is flowing. That is the concept. Beyond that, it is not much. One thing you have to watch out. Since '*ekamukhi*' and two face *rudraksha* are so rare—you know how greedy human beings have become in general—so normally, when you buy an '*ekamukhi*', it is a '*panchamukhi*' with face rubbed off and made to look like two or three. If you want to buy a genuine one, it is easier to buy a normal *panchamukhi*. That is what I suggest. If you have faith, then you can dip it in Manasarovar and use it but I will not advise most people

to use *rudraksha* for *japa* unless you don't care what happens. You can wear it, and then it kind of represents the protection of Shiva in his *rudra* form. *'Rudra' means* angry form—Aghora devata; that is what it means.

If a person who has some energy in him or her, who has some energy which is not normal, if he gives that to you, if you put it around your neck, that may have some uses. Certain things are useful, like a protection.

Basically, I used to have a *rudraksha*. Babaji used to have a *rudrakshamala*—huge *rudrakshamala*. People kept asking, wherever he went—he didn't go out much— but whenever he met people, they kept asking, 'Can we touch that *rudraksha*?' 'Will you dip this in water and give that water to us?' One day, I remember clearly that, we were sitting near the Bhagirathi near Gangotri. He got fed up, took out the *rudraksha* and broke it. I said, 'Stop, stop, I want one'. So he took one and gave it to me. He said, 'Whenever you want any connection with me, touch your chest with this *rudraksha* around your neck. Call me. Then one day, what I felt, you will feel. Throw it off.' So one day, many years after he passed away, in '85, I went somewhere and I was sitting and I said, what is this now, because people began to see this as *rudraksha*. I took it out quietly and let it go in the water. In those days, when I was wearing it, it helped me in some way to tune in. This is possible, but the person who gives it must be the person who knows what he is doing—not the priest who gives you the *mala* and says, 'Give 500 rupees!'

15

Satsang with Sri M

What is the use of rudrakasha mala for japa?

Japa with *rudrakshamala* is basically done by *sanyasins* and people who are inclined to the spiritual path. Others can use *sphatika* or *tulasi*, which are milder. You can do it but if something happens in your life which is terrible, it does not mean you should get confused. Your *bhakti* should remain. What happens usually with people is that *bhakti* remains as long as good things happen, when bad things happen they say what is this god I have been worshiping. They don't think that this may be part of a plan to wake me up. If you are surrendered that way, then *rudraksha* is okay.

Some people say, 'For tulasi there are many restrictions…'

That is because *Tulasi*, is associated with *Vaishnavites* but you can always use a *sphatika*. This is my personal understanding. If somebody who is known to you, has told you so for some reason which I do not know, but this is my personal understanding. *Sphatika* also you have to watch out; most of it is plastic or glass. *Sphatika* is a stone-crystal; supposed to be the water that is under the feet of Shiva. So Shiva's feet—Shiva and Shakti, both, are supposed to be there.

Are there supernatural lights visible in this region?

I would not say supernatural lights, I would rather say lights. There is some phenomenon happening there. It has been happening for years. There are some lights, that seem to come, touch and go. Now, these lights could be anything. Some people say they are *devatas* coming. Scientists say they are

some gaseous things going on. So that is not important to us. It is definitely—and those who have seen it say it is—a wonderful sight. You suspend your judgment as to what it is. If you see it, sit up, see it and enjoy it and if it touches you in any way, then you will find out for yourself.

Who was Padmasambhava?

The Tibetan region at one time was full of warring tribes. Tibetans at one time were totally wild—even the Chinese could not control them. Savage tribes fighting amongst each other. Their religion is called Bonpa. Followers of Bonpa religion (unlike the *shamans*, nature worshippers), used to go round and round and get into a trance, speak oracles and things like that. There was no kindness, no compassion, no nothing; no organised kind of religious practices. The Bonpas were used by kings to fight against other kings or to do black magic. One of the kings was called Trisong. Trisong was a civilized king, born in that savage terrain. He had heard about the teachings of Buddha from China but he knew that the origin of that was from India. So he sent somebody to Nalanda which was a centre of great Buddhist learning to invite a Buddhist monk to Tibet. They invited Shantasheela. Shantasheela was the first Buddhist monk to go there. He was a Theravada Buddhist, the original Uttarayana Buddhist, which is practised in Sri Lanka and Vietnam.

In fact, that is the original Buddhism—Mahayana came much later. Shantasheela was invited. He went and stayed

with King Trisong and tried to teach Buddhist teachings—some people were very happy with his teachings. He wanted to build a *gompa*. He could not do it because the Bonpas thought, he was a threat to their hegemony. So whenever he tried to build a temple they would break it down, apparently through black magic. Shantasheela said, 'I can't do anything about it because I am basically a pacifist, a Buddhist monk. I can't fight with these Bonpas; they seem to have some powerful connections.' So he suggested that in a place called Udhyan, which is now in Afghanistan there lived a monk, a yogi—matted haired, *jatadhari* yogi by name Padmasambhava—born of the lotus, they called him. He was a yogi, a tantric and a Buddhist, all in one. Shantasheela said, perhaps this guy may be able to handle the Bonpas. So Padmasambhava was invited and the story is that all along, as he came into Tibet, he was opposed by the Bonpas and he defeated them and built small gompas wherever he went. As he traveled, he stayed in many caves; they are called Padmasambhava caves, they are scattered all over Tibet up to Nepal. Padmasambhava was the first person to really establish Buddhism in Tibet. As he was a *tantric* and a Buddhist, the Buddhism that he established was coloured completely by Tantra; so there was worship of Tara and all that. That is what turned into Mahayana Buddhism. It was much later that the Dalai Lama came into the picture. The sect founded in his name was the oldest. They were called the 'yellow hats'—they wore yellow hats. They have written many books. They started translating all the Buddhist books

in Nalanda, which were in Pali and Sanskrit, into Tibetan. This was how the vast literature came. It was good because many of the books which we have lost are with them. They have been translated into Tibetan.

In Gangtok, if you visit the Rhotung monastery which belongs to a sect of Buddhists called the 'black hats'—followers of Milarepa, headed by the Karmapa—you will find a huge library which is full of palm leaf manuscripts. Some of the tantric texts, which have disappeared from India, can be found in Tibetan literature, including some which have not disappeared. Maha Nirvana Tantra is there in its original form. This is the story of Padmasambhava. They say in Mount Kailash too, there are places where he lived for some time. All these places are called caves of Padmasambhava. In fact the Buddhists call Kailash Kang Rinpoche. Rinpoche means 'precious jewel.' According to them, the great Buddha, Avalokiteshvara sits there on the top of the mountain. For them too it is very holy, which is why they do *namaskaram*—prostrate, get up, prostrate—and do *parikrama*, which is a nice way actually if you have time. It is a less tiring way of doing *Parikrama*, but you need time for it.

Why is Mount Kailash considered holy?

There must be something sacred about Mount Kailash. That is why it has been declared a holy zone; otherwise all mountains could have been declared holy. Besides, there is the existence of Manasarovar.

The head is the Kailash and the heart is the Manasarovar.

What is the need to keep 108 counts for japa?

This number 108 is given a special place because it is a multiple of nine. Nine represents *countlessness*. The energy is a constant factor in the universe. You cannot add to it or subtract from it. This is represented by the number 9. The most convenient multiple of 9 is 108. If you add any multiple of 9, you will still find the number 9. It is the only number which is like that. Any multiple—means 9 is a constantly existing element. Therefore it represents the constant-ness of energy. We come and we may go but the water will be flowing here. 108 is not a very large number and it is not a small number. It is a very convenient multiple of 9, therefore for chanting and protection it is used. If you say 1008 you will get horrified, so 108 is okay, but it is a multiple of 9.

Also, '*nava dwara*'. Dwarka is supposed to be the place where Sri Krishna lives. Door is derived from Dwara or a hole. So *navadwara* means the nine orifices or holes in the human system and therefore Dwaraka is the heart where Krishna sits, reigning over the land. Also *Navaratri-Navadurgas*, so 9 has always been given the importance and 108 is a convenient multiple.

Actually if you put your complete energy into chanting and even if you chant 109, nothing will happen. So don't get stuck on that but usually *malas* are made 108.

Please explain the reverence and devotion required during the parikarma.

I think you should not consider it as merely a picnic, which means, don't go around eating ice creams or throwing the sticks—that kind of thing. Have some reverence as you go around. Think that you are doing a sacred act and not just having a jolly good time. Anyhow by the time you do *parikrama*, you won't have enough energy to crack jokes but what I mean is, have a certain reverence for it. That's all. Keep a happy frame of mind. Don't get depressed because what happens in such groups is that if one person gets depressed, it spreads. So keep a happy frame of mind. Anyway I'll keep myself happy.

Om Shanti Shanti Shantih!

Satsang at Paryang

Bramhaanandam Parama-sukhadam, Kevalam Jnaana-murtim
Dwandvaateetam Gagana-sadrisham, Tattwamasyaadi-Lakshyam.
Ekam Nityam Vimalam Achalam, Sarvadhii Saakshi-bhutham.
Bhavaateetam Triguna-rahitam, Sadgurum Twum Namami.

So, we have gathered in Paryang. I was expecting that we would gather for *guru poornima* in Manasarovar. But we are not very far from Manasarovar; we are also in the vicinity of Mount Kailash. I think it is a wonderful occasion that we are all here for *guru poornima*.

Now, usually on *guru poornima* there is a full moon up there but it is too early here for the moon to come out. Today there has to be a full moon—the full moon is a symbol of *guru poornima*. The *poornima*—the full moon, is a symbol of something else: if that which it symbolises is there, then, our *guru poornima* is already celebrated!

'*Poornima*' means 'full moon'. It is actually a symbol of the cool light of the full moon that comes from the heart of a human being who has purified himself to such an extent that there is no cloud to hide the moon—this is the *poornima*. Why is it called *guru poornima*? That is because, usually, it is only the guru who has no clouds. Usually it is

the teacher who has no clouds and whose moon shines forth fully. This does not mean that others do not have a full moon shining forth. Actually, many people think that they are 'gurus'; but there might be some who never talk about it, but who may be having the full moon shining in the heart.

So, first, it is important to realise how one should be as a disciple before one can even think of being a guru. This morning, someone asked me, 'Today is guru *poornima*; how is the guru?' I said, 'As far as I am concerned, I am in top shape as a good disciple.' It has a certain implication. There was this man who went to a guru and asked him, 'I want to become your disciple; so what am I supposed to do?'

So the guru said, 'Meditate for six months, do this, do that.'

The man said, 'What does the guru do?'

The guru said, 'The guru just sits and gives instructions!'

So the man said, 'I want to become a guru!'

So everybody is ready to be a guru! You will find hundreds of people who are gurus by nature: they like to preach, they like to teach. But, what are they teaching when their moon is still covered with clouds? They mislead people, they end up in trouble. The greatest problem, the greatest bad *karma* that you can attract is to teach wrong things to people. They don't realise what they are doing—there is nothing worse than that. You have to be very careful of what you say, what you teach. Now, that is one aspect of *guru poornima*.

The other aspect is the guru himself and the relationship between the guru and the disciple. You all know that I hesitate

to call myself a guru, for the simple reason that it is difficult to get a good disciple. In fact, somebody asked me the other day, 'Is so and so also your disciple?'

I said, 'I have no disciples please, we are only friends.'

She said, 'We are your disciples.'

I said, 'Let us be friends.'

Why? Because, to say 'I am a disciple' is a very big commitment, a deep commitment. It is not easy, everybody cannot do that. So it is better to say, 'Yes, I know this person; I am related to this person.' Because, if you have become a good disciple, that instant you have become a teacher! So that is why serious teachers are always on the look out for good people. You don't need one thousand disciples; one is enough. That's why, when you sit down and scan people, you wonder if there is one somewhere, who might be able to do the job.

I told you the story of how I went to the Himalayas and my unsuccessful attempt to go to Kailash with my Master. He then told me, 'After some years, you will go to Kailash with lots of people.'

I was really terrified. I said, 'Why? Why? Why lots of people? Why can't I go alone?'

He said, 'You will have to teach.'

I was more terrified! 'Teach what?'

He said, 'You will learn afterwards.'

Somebody asked me the other day, 'What do these people do, staying alone in the Himalayas, doing nothing? They seem to be just living there and wasting their time; just doing noth-

ing.' I said, 'In my case, I know that this man whom I knew lived far away from society. The people who really knew him were the hill folk in certain villages, here and there. Nobody else knew him and yet he got certain things done. Just sitting quietly, 'doing nothing' is a great action which we cannot do in a hundred years. They find somebody, plant a seed and send them forth; they don't do anything... they just...'

I must tell you that my Teacher's direct Teacher, who is known in many places as 'Babaji' when I say 'Babaji' I am referring to my Master but there is a Babaji, who is my Master's Guru. My Master was a direct disciple of that Babaji. That Babaji is called 'Maha Avatar Babaji' by Yogananda Paramahamsa when he wrote the 'Autobiography of a Yogi'. He coined that term because he has been there for many years and he is doing so much work silently. In our tradition, nobody calls him 'Maha Avatar Babaji'. We call him, 'Sri Guru Mahadev' and 'Babaji'—only 'Babaji'.

In the tradition of *kriya* yoga, we call him Sri Guru. I have taught some people the *mantra*, *Sri Gurubhyo Namaha*. This is the *mantra* given in our tradition and Babaji has said, 'If you chant *Sri Gurubhyo Namaha*, you are instantly attracting my attention.' This was given to me by my Master, whom I call 'Babaji' whose real name was Maheshwarnath, because he belonged to the Nath Panth, before he came to Sri Guru Babaji.

Now, the relationship between a teacher and a disciple has to be so intimate that even fast friendships are not so thick. This is a relationship of absolute love and affection. Where correction is needed, one is very tough; but, at other times, it

is a relationship which, even your father or mother, husband or wife, or anyone else cannot give you. This is my experience. I may not be that good at it but I am talking about my experience with my teacher. When that kind of intimacy is there between a teacher and the taught, then gradually, by and by, the taught becomes the teacher. There is no need of doing anything—just the association and constant presence with the person, is enough. But then, that person must be that kind of a teacher. There are many kinds of teachers—even in school we have very good teachers, but, just because you go around with the teacher and make tea for him, you cannot learn geography! This is a different subject altogether.

When I used to wander with my Master, whenever he got tired—he never got tired! But I thought he was tired, having walked long distances in the mountains—I said, 'I'll massage your feet.' So I used to massage his feet. I used to think that I will massage his feet and put him to sleep but he never slept. I have never seen him sleep in my life. In the three and a half years I was with him, and the times I used go back and see him, off and on, I have never seen him sleep. When I went to sleep, he would be sitting before a *dhuni*. Wherever he went, he made sure, if possible, to have a *dhuni*. Every time I slept, my last image would be of him sitting straight, in front of the *dhuni*, staring into the fire. What he was looking at, I don't know. Or, he would be looking up there somewhere, eyes half closed—not closed also…

So, I used to massage his feet regularly. Usually, because I was only nineteen and a half years old and not accustomed

to all the toughness of mountain life, he used to give me a maximum of 20 kms a day to walk. After that, we would stop. Once we had to walk another 6 kms because there was no village or no place to rest in sight and finally we came to a cave, which he knew. He knew all the caves in the Himalayan territory. He said, 'We will stay here today.' So we climbed up—even climbing up to the cave was a big effort. We climbed up and he said, 'Light a *dhuni*.' By then, I had become an expert at lighting a *dhuni*! So I gathered some dry twigs and lit a *dhuni*. We sat down for a while. We had carried some *sattu,* flour. There was nothing else but some fruits. So we mixed some water from the Ganga into the *sattu* and ate it. We had the fruit, some guavas, which we had picked up on the way and then we decided to call it a day.

I was very tired. I began massaging his feet—it became a daily ritual. He said, 'Nahin, nahin! Tum, bacche, so jaao! I said 'Nahin, nahin,' and I carried on. I was so tired that while massaging, I didn't know when I fell asleep. I just dropped off and was fast asleep. In the middle of the night, I woke up. Something, I thought, was pulling my leg! In those areas, there are tigers—so my first thought was that 'Something is here, but where is Babaji? Usually, he is in front of me.' When I looked, the *dhuni* was there and I could see in the dim light, even though the flame was almost gone. I suddenly realized that my right foot was on his lap and he was massaging me! So I quickly got up and said, 'Babaji, what are you doing?' 'Aap kya kar rahe ho?' He said, 'Aré bacche so jao, aaraam se so jao.'

The other thing is that when he said, 'Aaram se so jao,' there was no way I could get up!

I am saying this to show the relationship between a guru and a shishya. That kind of intimate relationship is something very, very important to transfer what is in your heart into some other heart.

What I have been saying is also connected to the trip that we are taking here, at Kailash-Manasarovar, which is Sri Guru Mahadev Babaji's favourite haunt. More than Almora district and Badrinath area— which are also his favourite haunts—it is the Manasarovar-Kailash area that is his most favourite haunt.

There are many caves on the other side—we may not go through that side—where Buddhist monks are living. In some of those caves, Babaji, according to my Master, used to live for months together. So that is another reason for the sanctity attached to Kailash, for us, because that is the place where our root Teacher sits constantly, teaches constantly. I cannot guarantee that we will see him—I myself do not know.

Apart from our connection with Mount Kailash, Shiva who symbolises the principle of yoga, or the principle of meditation, or the supreme principle of *sadhana*, which takes us to the higher levels of consciousness, is supposed to have His abode on Mount Kailash. It is a symbol of that.

Apart from that, the Buddhists believe that Avalokiteshvara sits on top—for them also, it is a holy mountain. Besides that, as I said earlier, Padmasambhava, when he brought Buddhism into Tibet, spent many years in caves

near Mount Kailash and Manasarovar. Therefore, the Tibetans call it Kang Rinpoche. Kailash is called Kang Rinpoche, by the Tibetans because Guru Rinpoche—Padmasambhava is referred to as 'Guru Rinpoche'—stayed there for many years. He was the one who gave the Tibetans the mantra, *om mani padme huum*. In Sanskrit, it is *om mani padme huum* and in Tibetan, it is *om mani pamme huum*.

The other mantra which Guru Rinpoche taught, which we too can chant is *om vajra sattva huum*. This is the mantra which has a great effect on cleansing the body and the mind. In fact, our tradition deals with each individual in a different way—this is Babaji's teaching. I have given both these *mantras* to some people.

Om mani padme huum—means '*om* jewel in the lotus'. *Om* is the *pranava*, describing and showing all the levels of consciousness and vibrating through all the spheres—*om*.

Mani means 'jewel' and *padma* is 'lotus'.

So, *om mani padme hum* means 'Om jewel in the lotus'. The first book I wrote was called 'Jewel in the Lotus'. It is actually a Buddhist *mantra*. It is better not to say that it is Buddhist or Hindu or Christian; that is not our concern. Our concern is, is it effective or not? This is the mantra given by Padmasambhava, who is called Guru Rinpoche. 'Rinpoche' in Tibetan means 'precious jewel'.

So, since we will be going to Kailash, my *guru poornima* message is, first of all, keep the jewel in the lotus of your heart, clean and pure; don't allow anything to sully it! That means, don't have hatred towards anybody. Anybody! It doesn't

matter what people do. It's difficult, a tall order! 'Bless them that curse you'. You don't have to actively go and bless those who curse you, but at least, you can keep hatred out. Then your *mani* inside the *padma* will be very, very clean.

Secondly, we are going to a place which is equally holy and sacred for Hindus as well as Buddhists. The Tibetans also consider it a holy place and it is the abode of Shiva. You see how Shiva is depicted—He is the only God who is depicted sitting cross-legged, in *padmasana*, a yogic posture. Buddha also sits cross-legged. In fact, in the Western world, *padmasana* is called the 'Buddha pose' because Buddha has sat in *padmasana*.

Shiva therefore depicts the ultimate yogi, who sits on top of the hill, in *padmasana*, free of all other troubles, calm and peaceful, looking up, closing His eyes and opening the third eye, which is the eye of wisdom. That is the depiction of Shiva.

We have the mantra, *om namah shivaya*. As I told you, the real meaning of *om namah shivaya* is *shivo hum*. *Shivo hum* can be said only if the jewel in the lotus has been purified; otherwise, you cannot say, *shivo hum*. You can only say, *om namah shivaya* and bow down.

Om namah shivaya is called the *panchakshara*, not only in the northern tradition but also in the Shaivite tradition of the south. It is called the *panchakshara*, which means it has 5 letters - *na mah shi va ya* and depending on the combination of how you chant it, various effects can be produced in the human system. This is the effect of the *beejakshara*.

Now, a very effective one includes the energy of Shiva and also of Shakti, equally. Because everything has a positive and a negative aspect, it is like the anode and the cathode of a battery—both are equal, Shakti and Shiva! In fact, they say, 'Shiva,' without the 'ee,' the sound coming from letter 'i' of 'Shakt, becomes *shava* or 'dead body'. If you take out the 'i' from Shiva, then it will become *shava*. No effect! So that Shakti is there. The *beejakshara* for Shakti is *hreem*.

So a very beautiful Shiva mantra, which can be chanted as you go up and do the *parikrama*, is *om hreem namah shivaya*. You will find the effect of it. You don't have to shout aloud; all the energy will go in that shouting! In your minds, chant *om hreem namah shivaya*. Chant, if possible, fixing your attention at the navel, heart and top of the head. *Om hreem namah shivaya*.

You can also chant, *om mani padme huum*. *Om*, and the *huum* at the end, have a great effect on the psyche. Both can be chanted. You don't have to think, 'This is Hindu, that is Buddhist'—after all, the whole thing started from here, including Buddha and *Padmasambhava*. There is no difference.

Now, when you go to Mansarovar, from now on, whenever you are alone in your room, take ten minutes or half an hour out for yourself. Instead of constantly talking, sit quietly and meditate. Chant the *mantra* or just sit quietly and let your mind go within you. When you go to Kailash, you will be staying in tents. It is the best place to sit and meditate. You will see the difference.

In fact, it may be bad for the human body to have less oxygen, but it is great for meditation to have less oxygen! There is a simple reason for this, which has probably not been discovered. That the whole body is controlled by the brain everybody knows! There are many centres of the brain, that operate the parts of the body, and they require enough oxygen to do that. So, the maximum efficiency of the body depends on the oxygen that the brain receives. But there are other centres of the brain, which are to do with psychic activities, which function better when there is less supply of oxygen.

In *kriya* yoga, you breathe slowly. Actually, your oxygen content comes down, but you will not feel suffocated because that oxygen is enough to keep the functions of the body going. It also activates some other centres of the body, especially certain parts of the limbic system. It is near the limbic system, that you have the pineal gland and the pituitary. There is, according to us, a direct connection between the limbic system and the nostril, through a small thing called the amygdale, which comes here, between the eyebrows. That is why, when you chant *brahmari* that vibration of *brahmari* goes right up to there, through the amygdale.

So when there is less oxygen, it is a good time to meditate! This is why people go up in the Himalayas, sit in the caves and meditate. If you live there for many years, then the brain and the body get adjusted to living happily with that much of oxygen—like the Tibetans who live here. They don't need the level of oxygen that we do; they can function happily with

whatever oxygen there is in the atmosphere—but it takes time to adapt.

So, on this occasion of guru *poornima*, having said this much, I would like to invoke the blessings of Sri Guru Babaji, my Master Babaji, and all the great teachers who were before and who exist now, on all of us who are here, including those who don't know the language and who are around; those who are not listening to us; on all! One and all! I hope that some kind of spiritual evolution takes place in everybody's heart and soul.

I also pray to the great Energies that, somehow, we all go up and do successfully what we are supposed to do.

Now in this context, before I wind up, I want to thank all the people who have worked hard to organise this. We have to put up with all the little problems that we have, which are quite normal. When I used to walk around the Himalayas, there was nothing. There are people who go up walking, without any comfort at all. So, this is heaven! So excuse all the petty things.

I thank all of you who have organised this yatra. I don't want to name anybody but I especially want to say a word of thanks to our medicine man, who is traveling with us, who is so concerned about everybody that once or twice he comes up to me, very quietly, and consults and asks what to do. That shows concern. Concern is something which is a very spiritual matter.

Everybody has done something in some way—can't help it—saying all this. So there we are! Thank you very much and

I hope everybody goes and does whatever we are ready for. So what I suggest is, consider the yatra as a sacred act and spend some time everyday meditating, as we go closer and closer, on your own. Don't wait for me to come and sit there. That is what we are trying to teach, so that everybody does things themselves, not waiting for someone. I am sure that the blessings of the great teachers are with us. M is insignificant; a zero! But there are blessings coming!

Om shanti shanti shantih!
Om Namaḥ Shivaya!

Satsang at Manasarovar

So far we have come. Some people fell ill. Some people became alright. Today, I think, most people are kind of okay. I am hoping, by tomorrow, we will start the *parikrama* and by today evening most people will be ready to move. Now the fact is that your falling ill sometimes should not deter you. These things happen as long as the physical body is there. Little things happen to the physical body. They are actually little things. But they appear big. Because in our complex and luxurious surroundings, in the plains, where we always have the AC and the sun and the moon and whatever we want, are available. We don't realise the simplicity of life and how difficult it is. Once in a while, when we set out and face the difficulties which ordinary human beings go through, we get into trouble. That is it. There is nothing more. Then of course there is the fact that we come to a height where there is naturally a shortage of oxygen. Again, our lungs have gotten accustomed to such a surplus of oxygen down in the plains—now-a-days of course, mixed with diesel fumes—that the lungs find it difficult to get adapted to this rare level of oxygen. There are people like the Buddhist monks and so on, and *yogis*, who live in the higher ranges most of the time for whom this oxygen level is perfect. I think, when they come down, they feel a

little suffocated. The other way round. This is why they run back again.

Now having said all that, which is a matter of fact, about various things I want to tell you something, which is very important. We have come on a trip to Kailash. You can call it a trip or a pilgrimage, whatever you want. If you want to call it a pilgrimage, consider this trip to Kailash, this pilgrimage to Kailash, to be the same as our movement in day to day life towards Kailash—Kailash representing the lofty heights of truth; the lofty height at which truth sits. Mahadeva represents Truth. So, when you go on this pilgrimage, reflect on the matter, that in everyday life too we are on a pilgrimage. This is very true. If you look carefully, you will see what all travails you have to pass through, what all difficulties come your way. But then it is not in a short period of 17 days, so we don't look, actually we don't realise. It is stretched over a long time but is a pilgrimage. If you understand the fact that you are moving towards the lofty heights of truth, which is ice-clad, high up there, where the air is rarified, that is, only if you consider it as a pilgrimage. If you don't think so, if it is just fun, then it is ok, no problem. So let not this trip stop with having gone up and come back in one piece, which by the grace of whatever, we will do. But when we go back to Nepal, to Katmandu we should not say, 'back to the same grind'.

There is a pilgrimage ahead of us—the pilgrimage of life. And one is moving towards that which the Upanishads have declared, '*na tatra chakshur gacchati, na vaag gacchati, no manaha*'—where even the eyes do not reach, where words

cannot reach, which means, even descriptions do not suffice, which the mind cannot conceive. Now in a small way, this is what is happening to us. Our eyes actually, right now, cannot reach Kailash. I mean our eyes can only see it at a distance. Even when you do *parikrama*, we can still see it at a distance.

It is that which cannot be described or heard through words. Can you go home and describe the Manasarovar in its entire complete sense and make anyone understand? You can take photographs. That is a different story. You can show them a photograph. Or you can paint, if you are an artist. But is it the same thing? They have to come and see. What the *rishis* meant was that it has to be seen and understood. Even if it has been understood, it cannot be fully described. This is the internet world. Many of us, before we have come, we have googled. We have found the 'Kailash Yatra', we have seen the blue lake, and it is still not the same thing. This is different. You can actually go and touch the water. You can have a nice bath. Till I had a bath in the Manasarovar— it might be my imagination—I was having aches here and there, but I had a dip and everything has gone. Some credit should be given to the doctor's treatment. While trying to reach the unattainable, many descriptions fall short. There is a story of Shankaracharya. When he was traveling somewhere in the south, he came across a little child, who till the age of 9 had not spoken. He had not opened his mouth. Not a word. People thought Shankaracharya was a holy man, and was taken to the boy. The boy was sitting in a corner. Shankaracharya asked him, 'Why are you not speaking?' For the first time, the boy spoke. He said,

'About what?If I speak what I know, it will be untruth. The truth cannot be spoken.' Shankaracharya asked him, 'Are you ready to come with me?' The boy said, 'Why do you think I have been waiting here?' He got up and went with him. That boy was named Hastamalaka, Hasta Amalaka.

So this is what one is seeking. This pilgrimage is similar almost, because everyday we are uncertain. We don't know where we are going. We don't know what we are coming into. We fail to describe what is going on. Seeing it on internet is different from taking a dip in the Manasarovar. I am not telling anybody who has high fever to take a dip. Practicalities are different from reality, from absolute reality.

Consistently, the insistence is on finding the truth, to be going towards the truth. That word, truth, seems to be such an important word. Now what we have to think is just as in the pilgrimage of life, in this pilgrimage also it is good to be truthful. You have temperature? Be truthful. Say yes, I have. Don't show off. Feeling cold? Don't say I am not feeling cold. Now when you go back in the pilgrimage of life if you are seeking the absolute truth, is it possible to reach there, when 24 hours, you speak nothing but lies? People think that in life you can do anything you like. You can speak untruth, you can lie, you can murder, but if you read the book *'na tatra chakshur gacchati...'* you have reached the truth. This is not possible.

So in this pilgrimage of life stick to the truth as far as possible, especially in this journey. I am saying especially in this journey because we live in a world where everything is a lie. One company says this is the best car. You buy it. Another

company says that is the best car. Now who is telling the truth? Either both are telling the truth, which cannot be, or both are lying. Advertisements that we are exposed to, are lies. I am not saying 'lies' in the bad sense of the word, untruths or half truths. This is the world we live in.

So at least in spiritual matters, please don't tell lies. Don't say I meditated for six hours today and my lights were going up and down. Say only what you really feel. If you don't do so, that is the greatest blunder that can happen. Because then you are not being truthful, even in your own *sadhana*. How can one guide you? Is it possible, however hard one works? But one has to guide. One can't let go of anybody, once somebody is …

But you should also have a little kindness and imagine what amount of trouble we must be, to this guy. So at least in these matters, stick to the truth. And also, everyday when you get up in the morning, or go to sleep at night, look at yourself in the heart and say, 'Where am I? What am I doing? How many falsities have happened in my life? Even my *sadhana*, how much am I really doing?' People say I don't have time. We have time for everything. The urgency for *sadhana* has not arrived. If you have urgency to shit, you don't care how the bathroom smells, right? You can't stop it. So that urgency has not come. This is why we are not, nothing else. I am not saying we should artificially induce urgency. This is not possible. What happens is that we read in books that so and so has attained such a thing and we also hope to attain and for sometime we imagine that we are also attaining, but we are not. So what I am saying is, consider this.

One more thing in our relationship with the spiritual teacher—I won't even use the word 'spiritual'—in your relationship with the teacher, please be frank and truthful and clear. Don't try to bluff because it does not work. The teacher may not tell you that. But understands. So be very frank. I know some people can't do certain things because their wives object to it. Or their husbands object to it. So be frank:'Sir I did not do it because so and so happened.' Don't tell some other funny reason. It is not necessary. The teacher is not sitting there to grab anything from you. He has taken on a responsibility, reluctantly, with great pain. His master, put a responsibility on him. Otherwise it would have been beautiful. See that monastery up there. Everyday you can see the Manasarovar and Kailash. Food? Even the dogs get food. What is the big deal? Why are we wandering around and doing all this?

The third thing I will like to say is that spiritual development is not a mass affair. You cannot develop spiritually in groups. You are not sheep that can be herded together and made to eat the same food. Spiritual development is an individual affair. It is as if some groups can develop and some groups cannot. All that should be taken off from our minds. Here we should not have any groups. We should think of ourselves as human beings with another stupid human being sitting in front of us. There shouldn't be any groups. We have no groups.

There should not be any groups. Because the moment it comes in, we are differentiating ourselves from the whole. First differentiation starts by splitting ourselves into 'we are

this', 'we are that'. We breathe. We eat. We drink. We die. Common factor. In this there are no groups. So this is daily life. We follow this. This is like a pilgrimage. We are sitting here. Now we don't have groups here, do we? We are all one, going towards a particular goal, which is climbing. During the *parikrama* I can't say, I am this group, so I will not go with that group. In the same way, in day to day practice of living, don't have all that.

One more thing. No body has any monopoly on M. There is no such thing. As far as M is concerned, everybody is same. There is no monopoly whatsoever. If you understand this from the beginning, then you won't get hurt. Somebody is doing this. Why is it? Certain times, somebody needs to develop in some way. So people will be asked to do certain things. This person here does not need to be done anything. Nobody needs to do anything. After a few years, when I cannot walk, then may be, now I am ok.

These are real things about *sadhana*. I can sit here and quote from the scriptures and go on talking about that and this. I can do that, I am very good at that. But what is the use? Isn't it better to discuss matters concerning us? Or should we sit and chant "*urdhva mulam adhah shaakham…*" Nobody knows what it is. Now that I have said it, let me explain. It is in the 15th chapter of the Bhagawad Gita. If you go to the Himalayan monasteries and live for some time that's the first chapter you learn by heart because without chanting that, you cannot eat. You are not allowed to eat. Eating is the most important function. What if you are a *brahmachari*? You are

still hungry. So you have to learn it by heart because you chant it before you eat. So every *brahmachari* picks it up. Some people pick up in three months, I have seen, people who eat a lot. This is the 15th chapter called the Purushottama Yoga. Purushottama yoga starts with 'Shri Bhagavaan Uvaacha'—Krishna speaks. There are very few chapters in the Gita which start with 'Arjuna Uvaacha'. Most of them start with 'Bhagavaan Uvaacha'.

Urdhva-mulam adhah-shaakham
Ashvattham praahur avyayam
Chandhaamsi yasya parnaani
Yas tam veda sa veda-vit

The First *sloka* has so much built into it. It talks about a tree which you can't find anywhere here. All trees are not like this—its roots are up above and its branches are down below. It is an upside down, topsy-turvy peepal tree.

Anybody who has understood the leaves of this metaphorical peepal tree, which are down below, has understood all the '*chandas*' of the Vedas. He has understood the Vedas completely. The leaves and the branches in which various things are written, where the '*chandas*' of the Vedas is written, are the living beings and the earth, its mountains and rivers, and human beings and animals receive sustenance from up above because it is the root that is the source of sustenance. Basic sustenance of consciousness is received from up above. Therefore it is a topsy-turvy thing. Our roots are up above and in the human body it is the head.

In the ancient texts, anything that is described universally, in the macrocosm, will also be linked to something in the microcosm, which is the human system. In the human system, when this imagery is linked, the root is the head and the entire physical system is controlled by it. All sustenance is derived from this. If this stops any one function, that function suffers. Anyone who understands how these things function and how they are linked to the root, the head, is a yogi. He has understood the Vedas. Therefore self-realization means, to first understand the connection between the body and the brain. Not to say that, I am the supreme Brahman. You are not. Actually not, in day to day existence. The connection between the root and the branches—how are they linked? A clear understanding of anatomy and physiology is an important aspect of yoga. That is the first realisation of yourself; first understanding of yourself. I am not saying you should all do medicine, but this is biology. You need not go into details—but a general understanding of this is necessary. You may now understand why yoga prescribes certain respiratory systems, certain levels of breathing, and certain rhythms, certain postures. If your consciousness was not linked to the physical organism, what is the use of all this? Therefore that root of the *ashwatha* tree, which is the head in the human system, is called Kailash where Mahadeva sits. And the main trunk is the spinal cord. And the nerves which radiate are the branches. The organs to which they reach out and operate are the leaves. And the different centres where certain operations take place are the *chakras*. This is merely a cluster of nerves, called the plexus.

According to our *parampara* of '*Kriya*' this whole system of world is linked within the body. All pilgrimages are performed within Kailash being on the top. So when we do the *parikrama*, when we go on this pilgrimage, we should also remember, we are also paying homage to Mahadeva, who is sitting within. We are carrying that with us all the time. Give a little attention and consideration to the sacredness you are carrying. Once in a while think. You are not merely a bundle of flesh and bones.

Om Shanti Shanti Shantih!

Satsang at Nyalam

Satsang at Prayang on Gurupoornima

Satsang at Prayang – Sri M making a point

Yatris posing with Sri M at Mansarovar before commencing the return journey

Tents pitched on the banks of Mansarovar

On the way to Saga

Our tents at the foot of Mt. Kailash

Sri M during the trek

Sri M at the foothill of Mt. Kailash

(Facingpage) Arduous trek up to Dolmala Pass

Yatris in a trail

Walkers with Sri M

Yamadwar – the gateway to Kailash parikrama

Yatris commencing the parikrama with the blessings of Sri M

Diverse faces of the holy Mt. Kailash

Mansarovar – a picture of peace and serene beauty

Sri M on the bank of Mansarovar

Preparing for a dip in Mansarovar

A stop on the way to Saga

An idyllic view of the mountains and the plains

Sri M during the trial trek in Nyalam

A trial walk in Nyalam